HELPING THE DEPRESSED

A SPURGEON'S BOOKLET

# Helping

# the

# Depressed

**ALISTAIR ROSS**

Series Editor
Paul Beasley-Murray

KINGSWAY PUBLICATIONS

EASTBOURNE

*Cover artwork by Ron Bryant-Funnell*
*based on an original design by John Herbert*

**British Library Cataloguing in Publication Data**

Ross, Alistair
    Helping the depressed.
    1. Counselling
    I. Title
    361.323

    ISBN 0-86065-876-7

Printed in Great Britain for
**KINGSWAY PUBLICATIONS LTD**
1 St Anne's Road, Eastbourne, E Sussex BN21 3UN by
Richard Clay Ltd, Bungay, Suffolk.
Typeset by Nuprint Ltd, Harpenden, Herts.

# Preface

Founded in 1856 by the Victorian 'Prince of Preachers', Charles Haddon Spurgeon, Spurgeon's College is an evangelical Baptist theological college located in south London, which over the years has trained many hundreds of men and women for Christian leadership both in the UK and overseas. Spurgeon's has always had a strong emphasis on vocational as well as academic training. It is only natural therefore that, with Kingsway Publications, Spurgeon's, under its Principal Paul Beasley-Murray, has teamed up to produce this present series of booklets, which aim to cover a wide variety of pastoral issues.

Before becoming Principal of Spurgeon's in 1986, Paul Beasley-Murray served with the Baptist Missionary Society in Zaire (1970–72) and for thirteen years was Pastor of the Baptist Church in Altrincham, Cheshire (1973–1986).

# Contents

# Introduction

Another day dawned, and like the days before, for Rachel they seemed dark and despairing. Rachel struggled to get out of bed. Last night she had lain awake for hours longing for the release of sleep to come. Yet in what seemed a few moments another day had arrived. Lifting the duvet was exhausting. Minutes slipped by and Rachel found herself still on the bed, still unwashed and undressed. 'Why bother when nobody cares?' she wondered as she struggled into the same dark, sombre clothing she had worn the day before and the days before that. Breakfast was a mechanical affair, the cornflakes tasting little better than the packet they had come out of.

Waiting at the bus-stop Rachel thought to herself, 'Why not end it all? No one would notice if I threw myself under a bus.' Rachel suddenly found herself sitting on the bus not knowing how she got there. She dreaded recognising anyone she knew and would have to talk to as it required so much energy.

Rachel simply wanted to be alone and began to avoid her friends in case they asked how she was and saw through her reply. Inside it all felt such an effort but on the outside she continued to smile and plod on with her job. 'Where is God in all this?' she thought. 'As a Christian I am meant to believe in him but he doesn't hear me, too busy listening to other prayers from "good" Christians, I suppose. They deserve his attention, not me. I'm so tired I just want to fall asleep and never wake up.' Rachel struggled through the day's work and struggled home again without anyone noticing how depressed she had become. Behind her smiling face was an aching heart. A day came when the pretence, the tiredness and the numbness became too much and Rachel was forced to get the help she so badly needed.

Rachel was suffering from depression, although if you had asked her friends they would have been most surprised. Symptoms of the depression were influencing her thinking, her emotions and feelings, her daily life and her faith. She had become a pale shadow of her former self but told nobody because she did not think anyone would understand. Instead, she wrote these words:

> She stood before the mirror.
> Pain-glazed eyes stared back
> Dull and lifeless
> Mirroring the soul within.
> Stroke by stroke the make-up is applied:
> Mask of deception skilfully covers.
> Morning is here: and so again

> The broken hearted clown
> Faces her audience to give
> The finest of performances.

If Rachel was sitting in your lounge, office or study, talking to you because you are her friend, home-group leader, elder or pastor, how would you help her?

Rachel is a real person and all the stories and comments that are made in this book are by real people with real experiences of depression. For the obvious reason of confidentiality their names and some of the situations have been changed. I was asked to see Rachel by her pastor. As we talked about what was troubling her, Rachel talked about the death of her mother. When I suggested that she seemed very angry about this and other events in her life, which her mother's death had brought sharply into focus, Rachel exploded, and shouted, 'I am not an angry person.' We agreed to carry on talking about these issues on a regular weekly basis and Rachel went to her GP, who gave her a short course of antidepressant drugs.

There are others, like Rachel, who have a personal faith in God and regularly attend church, who do not always find the help or care they need or deserve. In a questionnaire sent to a number of Christians I knew to have been depressed, one of the questions was 'What help did you receive from your spouse, family, GP, church, psychiatrist or anyone else?' One young mother replied 'none' for each of these, even though she had suffered from post-natal depression with her second child.

Although depression has been around as long as the human race and at some stage every one of us has been touched by it, there are many for whom depression is as painful, isolating and serious as that described by Rachel. Where do they turn? Who can they ask for help? Is there anyone who will really understand the vulnerability and pain that they feel?

This book is written with the aim of helping Christians to care for the depressed by:

(i)  increasing our knowledge and understanding of depression;

(ii)  exploring what depression feels like;

(iii)  seeing in what practical ways we can begin to help; and

(iv) answering some of the questions that depression raises for Christians.

# I

## *Signs of Depression*

Depression is a common but complicated condition, difficult to define, hard to describe with accuracy, and not easy to treat.' [1] Someone I know had actually been depressed and not realised, until months later they described that period of their life to a doctor.

When the doctor said they had been suffering from depression, it came as a revelation, and made a great deal of sense of what they had been through. One reason for this reluctance or difficulty in recognising depression is that people feel a failure or as if they are letting God down.

So if depression is so common and so difficult to define and people are reluctant to admit to being depressed, how do we recognise a depressed person? There is a whole range of factors that give us clues as to whether or not a person is depressed. These factors need to be taken as a whole and are simply a rough indicator that all is not well.

Remember Rachel, the women sitting in your

lounge? As she unfolds her story, hesitantly, and with many silences, there are four noticeable pointers that indicate she is depressed and not just feeling out of sorts or having a bad day.

## 1. Exhaustion

Rachel had trouble sleeping, and even simple tasks like getting out of bed or making breakfast were draining. While we all have trouble sleeping on occasions, we rarely experience the sense of overwhelming tiredness that depression can bring.

## 2. Emptiness

Even though Rachel's days were busy and she managed to carry on working for a few months, it meant little to her. She felt she had achieved nothing, there was no satisfaction in even struggling through a day. For Rachel life seemed a succession of empty non-events. Life was a matter of existence. As she described her life to me it seemed like an empty, barren desert with little hope of survival.

## 3. Experiences of despair

Finding herself alone in this 'desert' soon led Rachel to feel like giving up on life. Consequently, it didn't matter what she looked like or what she wore. Nobody cared for her (or so she thought). The negative way she viewed herself affected her thinking and her feelings. 'Nobody cares, but why should they about someone like me? Who would want a friend like me? I certainly wouldn't.' Rachel felt a deep sense of despair that nothing would ever change.

## 4. Escape

Rachel had lost any perspective about the future. She existed in the grim reality of the present from which she wanted to escape. None of us knows what the future holds but we generally have a fairly balanced and hopeful outlook. We may be looking forward to a holiday, getting a new car, moving to a new house or going to a party.

Depression robs us of this future perspective. All the future holds is bleakness and despair. So a helpful question to ask Rachel was, 'What are you looking forward to?' Rachel said that there was nothing that made her life worth living. The most logical, and at the time, the most seemingly rational solution was to commit suicide. We will be dealing with this important subject at a later stage. Rachel simply longed to lie down and never wake up. Elijah also experienced exhaustion, despair and expressed suicidal thoughts after his success on Mount Carmel (1 Kings 19).

If a person is experiencing difficulties in any of these areas it is a sign that they might be depressed and need help. As well as these indicators that we have seen in Rachel's life there are others we can observe.

## 5. Slowing down

The person slows down both in their activity and their thinking. It becomes difficult to concentrate and make decisions. Their memory becomes poor and the normal motivation and drive fades. What was once done as routine now becomes difficult. The person becomes increasingly irritable and even their body moves slowly and doesn't have the energy it once did. Other people find the opposite problem of becoming agitated or restless. They cannot settle to anything, concentration is difficult, trivial incidents get blown out of proportion and everything sets the person on edge.

## 6. Changing patterns

We all have patterns in our sleeping, eating and in our sexual relationships. As depression develops, these patterns become disturbed. A depressed person may have no problem getting to sleep, but despite being very tired may wake in the early hours of the morning and be unable to get back to sleep or may just doze fitfully. At its simplest level there are two major types of depression; more will be said about this in Chapter 4. With one form of depression, the person feels exhausted and just can't get going first thing in the morning, but their mood improves as the day goes on. With the other form the person tends to feel worse as the day goes on and by the evening may have slowed almost to a stop.

A depressed person can lose all appetite. Even

favourite food becomes tasteless. Weight simply falls off and the person can reach a stage where their lack of energy is in part because they are not eating enough to sustain the body's demands. Others who are depressed try to find comfort in food. They then become overweight which in turn gives them another reason for looking negatively at themselves.

People who are depressed lack enthusiasm for things they normally enjoy, such as shopping, reading, watching TV etc. Sex can also become a problem as they feel they have not got the desire, the energy or interest in physical sexual expression. Often this is misunderstood by their partner as rejection or it raises questions about the rest of the marriage. Unless this is understood the person who can best help is left feeling isolated and sometimes hurt.

## 7. Tears and fears

When human beings are in emotional or physical pain they cry and the tears roll down the cheeks. One of the most poignant verses in the Bible is 'Jesus wept' (Jn 11:35). As a person becomes increasingly depressed they find that they cry for no apparent reason. Sitting in a church service, watching a TV programme, a kind comment from a friend and before they know it they are bawling their eyes out. The tears flow from a deep, unhealed wound of sadness within (Ps 6; 42:3).

As well as tears there may be increasing feelings

of anxiety or fear. People believe they are 'cracking up' and do not know what to do about it. They become frightened of unusual physical symptoms like their heart racing, their stomach churning over, sudden dizziness or overwhelming feelings of panic.

## 8. Out of perspective

A depressed person thinks that they are the only one with this problem. They no longer have any confidence in themselves and are afraid to tell anyone else. Such a person withdraws from others, sensing that they are rejecting him or talking about him behind his back. Christians often feel guilty about some past sin that they now feel they are being judged for. God seems remote and uncaring, as the person is unable to pray or read the Bible.

A more serious sign is if the person starts hearing voices. Sometimes these voices tell them to end it all, and suicide is seen as a perfectly sensible answer to their problems.

## 9. Disturbed thinking

Most of us day-dream and imagine past events with fond memories. Our brain records all these memories and, like a computer, if the right keys are pressed, we are able to recall them. Sometimes our past contains painful memories that we don't want to recall. When a person becomes depressed this seems to upset the way we recall memories and they can come flooding back in a way we cannot control.

This is a frightening experience that can intrude into our daily life. We can also become obsessed by a recurrent thought or memory. It leaves many people feeling that they are about to 'crack up'.

## 10. Aches and pains

Everyone experiences aches and pains but when someone is depressed there is a whole range of physical symptoms which are their body's way of saying that something is wrong. These include constipation, backache, headaches and a dry mouth. A person can become tense and agitated which in turn can also result in a tight chest, breathlessness, a pounding heart and shaking.

If we are helping someone who we think may be depressed, by asking ourselves some simple questions, and listening carefully, we can gain a fairly clear idea if they are depressed. It would be helpful to suggest that they visit their local GP as we are not doctors and are not in the business of making medical diagnoses.

* Do they feel unusually tired, especially guilty or unable to make simple decisions?
* What do they feel about life at the moment? What do they think God feels about them?
* Are they easily upset, tearful or short-tempered?
* What are they looking forward to?
* Have they ever thought about suicide or made any plans about it?

Listen and observe. Take note of the way they are dressed, their eyes, whether they look at you, their facial expressions and the way they sit or stand. Also note sighs, groans and the length of time it takes for them to respond to a question or volunteer information. Beware of the person who copes well with life and who smiles on the outside but whose heart can be aching inside. The answers they give to questions like those above can help us see if they are depressed even if they don't look it. All this information helps you to build up a whole picture of the person you are trying to help. Finally ask yourself this question, 'Does this person make me feel depressed?' What a person feels like when they are depressed is important and is the subject of the next chapter.

# 2

## *Describing Depression*

A young woman finding out that she was unable to
have children went into a 'Deep depression which,
as someone who has never been subject to great
heights or depths, was distressing in the extreme.'
Trying to communicate to others what depression
feels like is no easy task.

One way that I use is to get the person to draw
how they feel on a large piece of paper with felt
pens. Instead of having to rely on words, the draw-
ings are able to show what is going on within the
person. Another way is to get the person, if they are
able, to put down on paper what it is they feel. So
often people who have great difficulty in commu-
nicating verbally can express eloquently and artis-
tically the terror, isolation and the pain that
depression holds for them. Some of these pictures,
poems and words even in their pain hold out that
somehow there is hope. For people who are Christians that hope is rightly centred on God, who in
this apparent abandonment is still there. Nothing,
not even depression, can in reality 'Separate us

from the love of Christ' (Rom 8:35–39). There are six main images that have been used to describe depression.

First, there will be images of isolation and separation. Very often there will be small figures behind walls, surrounded by black oppressive clouds or fog. Sometimes the person is surrounded by towering walls or barriers, like some prison. There will be endless tunnels where all that can be drawn is a gaping, all-consuming mouth that threatens to engulf for ever. One drawing showed a person marooned on a desert island surrounded by sharks. Here are some words that depressed people have used to describe their experience.

> My heart is breaking with hurt, hands bleeding from hammering on the wall that will not break down to see the love they tell me is on the other side.

The very ground on which the person stands seems to give way and become a pit in which they are imprisoned:

> I am in a pit. I have reached rock bottom. God has come and pulled me onto a ledge, and I must stay here until he pulls me up.... Some time has passed. I thought I had crawled out of the pit, only to find I had slipped back into its grip.

> > At first unseen, Creeps the fog,
> > Lightly skipping over the soul,
> > Curling gently, Clinging lightly,
> > Insidious first sign of the darkness to come.
> >
> > Then sighted,
> > Thickening slowly around the heart,

Gripping more closely, Encompassing firmly,
Emotions die, As the darkness deepens.

Sight fails at last,
Far objects—future—cannot be seen,
Only the eerie silence, Thoughts and
memories, mingled in swirling confusion.
The isolation is complete.

Such a sense of isolation often prevents a
depressed person from asking for help. They justify
this by saying things like 'No one will understand,'
'People will think I am mad.' This sense of isolation
stopped Rachel, who wrote the above poem, from
getting help for several months.

Secondly, images representing a deep hurt or
wound. People draw themselves with limbs miss-
ing, displaying open wounds, sometimes ripped in
half or headless, in an effort to convey their pain.
One elderly lady drew a beautiful tree full of life,
birds and squirrels. When asked what she saw in
her picture she pointed to a black patch near the
base of the trunk and replied, 'The tree may look
healthy but its heart is dead and it can give life no
more, it is waiting to die.'

One girl wrote in a prayer to God, 'I've cried out
for relief from the ripping apart that goes on
inside…my God don't play games.'

So strange, living with raw pain of the emotions. Were
it a physical pain, you could seek for a course of
treatment and at least have painkillers…but how
does one live with emotions ripped open, torn and
bleeding? How does one smile, and function, when
you cannot understand how others cannot see the

gaping wound? What painkillers reach the soul, the spirit?

Thirdly, there are a variety of images often representing the feeling of despair. One person drew an amazingly complicated maze in which there was no way out. That's what depression feels like. Despair says 'One can only bleed so long before one dies.' One powerful image was that of a hunted animal:

The hunted animal, tired from the long running, cowed in the corner, with all the dogs of Hell snapping at her heels. Fear and panic have paralysed her—she can run no further. There is nowhere to hide...with her last strength she will drag herself on another inch, another yard, spirit broken by the chase, body exhausted by the strength-sapping miles she has come, running with a power she does not possess until all life has drained away.

> Stark terror
> Hidden
> In her rigid
> Body
> Wide eyed
> The tiny rabbit
> Strains
> At every sound.
> Ensnared, confused
> Foot crushed
> By rusty teeth
> Hears the approach
> Of hunters steps
> From the East
> Fox's stealth
> From the West

> As in the darkness
> She awaits her fate.

Fourthly, another powerful image, often linked to anger, is that of destruction.

> At times I feel as if my mind is an unexploded bomb: yet the timer is uncertain. Or a volcano—sometimes dormant, sometimes ready to explode in red-hot pain—it must be controlled—the risk is too great.

This fear of destruction makes the person try to hold in the pain and feel that any attempt to relieve the pressure is too dangerous.

Fifthly, like the aftermath of a nuclear holocaust, the image of barrenness is often depicted. Mary drew hearts to describe her depression. One was white with a few coloured patches within it. For Mary this was the worst she had ever been as the white was a coldness that had all but frozen any life out of the heart. Another was black with a gold centre, signifying some hope, however small.

> Twisted, scarred
> Monstrous travesty
> Of created potential
> Barren remnant
> In a barren landscape
> The lightning tree—
> Symbol of death.
> Yet, from its root
> Still in the darkness
> Springs a shoot
> Which may yet
> Grow into the light.

Sixthly, there are images of death and hell. These appear to be particularly strong for those with a personal faith.

It seems as though the pit of hell was opened up and I have looked in and what I have seen has filled me with terror I could never imagine. I want only the light: see only the darkness. I want only life: see only death and destruction.

It is helpful for us to know as much as we can from the pictures and words that those suffering from depression produce. It is not always an easy process as some of the images produced are quite disturbing. It is encouraging when there is some sense of hope—even if unexpressed. There is always the danger of reading too much into pictures and images. So it is important to let the person who has produced them say what they see in them.

Given the bleakness of many of these images, is there any hope for people with depression? The word of God and the people of God say 'yes'. The Bible's emphasis, while acknowledging the depths of human despair, is on the certainty of God's commitment to us 'and the assurance of abundant life in heaven if not on earth. Paul's confident prayer for the Romans will someday be answered for all Christians... (Rom 15:31).' [2]

## Further reading

Dorothy Rowe, *The experience of depression* (John Wiley: Chichester, 1978).
Noreen Riols, *Eye of the Storm* (Hodder and Stoughton: London, 1983).

# 3

## The Causes of Depression

Children have the delightful ability to ask simple, obvious questions that require complex answers, such as 'Daddy, why is the sun hot during the day and cold at night?' An obvious question to ask about depression is 'What causes it?' This too has a complex answer. Depression is caused by a number of physical and a number of psychological factors and sometimes a combination of both.

### The physical causes of depression

Firstly, there are genetic and hereditary factors. At the moment of conception a life is formed, with a unique genetic blueprint. By this is determined features, like, sex, the colour of eyes and temperament. Babies are born with the basic building blocks of personality already in place, although these will be shaped and moulded by childhood and adolescence. This means that some people inherit a personality more sensitive to psychological causes of depression, such as rejection or loss. Similarly, research has also suggested that people can inherit a chemical vulnerability to depression. In some people the delicate chemical balance within the brain is more easily 'tipped' than others and depression is the result.

Secondly, there are biochemical factors. The brain is a complex and intricate mechanism, which operates by the transmission of minute electrical impulses along chains of nerve cells. This transfer is done chemically by neurotransmitters. Studies have suggested that if the chemical balance of the neurotransmitters becomes disturbed, depression can result.

Another biochemical change which is linked to depression is the level of hormones in a person's body. A woman experiences this as part of her menstrual cycle. Premenstrual tension (PMT) is increasingly recognised as a genuine problem for many women and this is often accompanied by depression. These hormonal changes also explain why many mothers become depressed shortly after the birth of their baby. The balance of two hormones is now altering and two other hormones that are unique to pregnancy are no longer being produced.

Studies have shown that endocrinal and hormonal changes, as well as zinc deficiencies, produce depression in some women. Other studies suggest that there are certain groups of people who are more prone to depression, primarily for psychological reasons. Those at greater risk include: women over thirty, those who are unmarried, those with an unwanted pregnancy and women who already have problems relating to mental illness.

Similarly, a number of women become depressed at the time of the menopause, where the body no longer produces certain hormones. However there may also be important psychological reasons— such as, the feeling of no longer being a 'proper' woman—why this time in a woman's life may produce depression.

Thirdly, there are a variety of physical causes that may produce depression, such as head injuries, viral infections, epilepsy and haemorrhages. Jack went into hospital for a heart bypass operation. Quite out of character he became depressed, even though the operation was successful. He lost interest in everything, became tearful and thought he would never recover. The surgeon explained to him that this was fairly common after his type of operation. Several days later, Jack found his mood changing and could now see that after time for recovery he could lead a normal life again.

## The psychological causes of depression

From a vast number of psychological factors that can contribute to an experience of depression, there are a number of key issues that recur again and again.

### The past in the present

What happens to us in the past often has an influence on the present. Wordsworth understood this when he wrote, 'The child is the father of the man.' Our brain records all our thoughts and feelings and they are deposited in our unconscious. Although we are not always able to recall them, they can have a pervasive effect and can account for depression now.

The early months of a baby's life are a critical time for the future development of that baby. This fragile baby has needs and they are a great deal more than feeding one end and changing the other!

The skin contact, cuddling, holding, feeding, changing and sounds made by a mother to the baby build the relationship. A bond is established where the baby has learnt to trust this person who meets all its needs, however inarticulate the cry that communicates that need.

As the baby grows into a toddler and then a young child, it learns from the adults around it. A child learns by what its parents say. If a child hears 'Who's the most gorgeous baby in the world?'; 'Isn't he the cleverest boy you've ever seen?' then they tend to believe it. If the adults are negative in their comments, 'What a pity it's another girl'; 'Mummy doesn't love a bad boy'; then there is a fair chance the child will believe them.

Children also need to know that they are loved and that can be expressed in two important ways. Firstly, children need time. Time to tell you all about the ups and downs of their day, who said what in the playground, what they feel about their teacher and how they hate their best friend because she sat next to someone else that day. They need to know that you have time to play with them, read them a story, pretend that you are a cowboy or an Indian. Secondly, children need to feel accepted and loved through physical contact. They like hugs and kisses, to be whirled around or turned upside down in daddy's arms and to sit on a mother's knee.

All human beings need a basic sense of trust, communicated by bonding, a basic sense of value, communicated by the words we use, and a basic sense of being loved, communicated by time and touch. However, parents are fallible and human, and often can only give what they themselves have received. They respond in a similar manner to the way they received time, love, affection and care from their parents. If they lack in any area they do the best they can, but for many this is uncharted waters and there is a constant danger of shipwrecks. One consequence of a person's past is that their experience of depression as an adult can be linked to one of these basic needs not being met, or not as fully as that person wants.

*Depression in the family*

Depression is contagious. If someone grows up in a family where a parent is depressed this can have a variety of influences. They may absorb, in an unconscious way, the way parents act and react. Certain subjects may become taboo and the fact of depression may be denied: 'Mummy is feeling a bit unwell today, we've got to be very good for her.' 'Don't do that; it gives daddy one of his headaches.' Another influence is that a family member may begin to think negatively about themselves. 'If only I was a better boy or girl my mum or dad wouldn't feel so bad. If I was a nicer person, daddy would not be in such a strange mood.' Children can think that all that goes on in a family is due to them. They can take all the burdens of the family on their tender and ill-equipped shoulders. Everything that happens is their fault and it leaves them thinking badly about themselves. Often their own needs are neglected and their own feelings are repressed as they try to be 'strong' or 'good' for everyone else. As an adult this can be seen in the low esteem or the level of self worth they attach to themselves.

The depressed family can also encourage negative thinking. This type of thinking includes such ideas as: a perfectionist 'all or nothing' attitude; it always looks on the black side of things; it makes sweeping generalisations; minimises the importance of good things and jumps to unwarranted conclusions.

*Loss and rejection*

When a person loses something or someone very important to them they frequently become depressed. It feels if part of them is no longer there and can produce feelings of rejection, loneliness, isolation and abandonment. The most obvious loss is the death of someone who is loved. When someone has been bereaved they pass through a time of shock and overwhelming emotional pain to reach a point of anger and depression. 'If only the ambulance had come more quickly' is one comment

34

that illustrates how this anger is focused. This is a natural part of the healthy grieving process. A person can get 'stuck' and remain depressed, unless some help is given. Other significant losses include the death of a pet, separation and divorce that brings about similar deep feelings.

Paul was six years old when his parents moved to the USA. Despite all the excitement of the new life, Paul longed to go back to England. He especially missed his grandparents. The sense of excitement soon paled and the sense of loss grew to the extent that Paul was exhibiting all the signs of depression, which is rare in a child. When Paul's family returned to England, Paul's depression disappeared over a period of time.

Loss is not always about relationships. In the course of life people invest themselves in what they do, and so if these things come to an end or are lost there is a traumatic response seen in depression. It may be a career, a football match, their health, a house or a special possession. One woman whose safety deposit box had been stolen said, 'My life was in that box.'

The depression that loss, separation, rejection and loneliness may produce can stem back to events in the early months of life. However the losses are traumatic enough in themselves to cause depression.

*Hurt, anger and forgiveness*

Everyone gets hurt. Part of being human is to live in a far from perfect world, full of far from perfect people. On average four-hundred and thirty-six children get hurt every day just through the divorce of their parents. What is important is what we do with that hurt. Hurt can often result in feelings of anger. Anger about the way a person has been treated, used or let down. Sometimes that anger is turned inward and the person who has been let down feels that they are responsible, it was really their fault or they feel guilty for having such strong feelings. Many Christians are ashamed of feeling angry and often do not know what to do.

Lucy felt depressed and so went to her pastor. He rang me and asked if I would be able to help her. After spending an hour listening to Lucy it became clear that depression was only the surface problem. I said that I felt she was a very angry person, which she angrily denied! Over the following weeks this subject came up again and again until she felt able to tell me about the cause of her rage.

Lucy's depression was clearly caused by her inability to deal with anger. She felt that if she expressed it she would destroy herself and others, and so at all costs she must keep it under control. But all the time it was burning away inside like some smouldering fire. Frozen rage or repressed anger is often expressed in depression.

The feelings of hurt and anger also raise the question of forgiveness. Jesus knew that our need of forgiveness was vital and this is one reason why he went to the cross. In following Jesus, the ongoing place of forgiveness is stressed (Eph 1:17; Col 1:13–14). Many Christians know the words 'Forgive us this day our trespasses, as we forgive those who trespass against us' (Lk 11:14) but find it difficult to do, or have difficulty in forgiving themselves.

Julie had experienced depression since the birth of her first child. Although that was several years before, she was still depressed. We began to explore what the depression was all about. Over a period of time it became clear that Julie had always had a poor relationship with her mother. In fact it seems that Julie was an unwanted child and over the years she had felt this built up a real hostility to her mother. Time and again we came back to whether or not she could forgive her mother for depriving her of the love that she so desperately needed. There were other aspects to the depression, but as Julie felt able to express her anger and lack of worth and not be rejected, she also found the ability to allow the Lord to help her forgive her mother. Julie's depression did not disappear overnight but it was a turning point.

Forgiveness is easy in theory. But when we have been hurt by someone we have to be willing to let go of the hurt, and that is hard to do if we have been clinging on to it for a long time. If we do not let go, bitterness can grow up in our life. Like some cancer, it gnaws away on the inside, spreading throughout our mind and capable of destroying it. Forgiveness is not always a once for all act. It can be a process of letting go when painful memories are aroused.

*Traumatic events*

Rape and child abuse are perhaps the most traumatic events that happen to anyone. Even as I write this I feel pain for those whom I have counselled whose lives have been damaged in this way. Proverbs raises the question, 'A man's spirit sustains him in sickness but a crushed spirit who can bear?' (Prov 18:14). A number of examples quoted in this book have been individuals who have been sexually abused. In their case the depression was just the tip of the iceberg. All who have been made victims in this way may have to struggle with depression. They will have lived with negative thinking, shattered trust, distorted affection, red-hot anger and rage, profound rejection and isolation.

Obviously they need specialised care and counsel as depression is often the 'mask' that hides even deeper wounds.

*Unhelpful teaching*

While the Christian faith does not cause depression, there are aspects of biblical teaching which if misunderstood can contribute to a person's depression. This includes: an unhealthy emphasis upon sin; a conditional expression of love; a certainty that leaves no room for doubt; an unwillingness to recognise emotional problems; an embargo on anger; and a shallow understanding of forgiveness. On the other hand there is also the opportunity to provide a care and concern that is deeply practical and touching, the willingness to accept people because Christ accepts them, the belonging of a family, the support through teaching, relationships, worship and the presence of the Holy Spirit that enables lives to be healed and rebuilt to the glory of God (2 Cor 5:17).

## Further reading

Mary Pytches, *Yesterday's Child* (Hodder and Stoughton: London, 1990).

# 4

## A Medical View of Depression

A doctor or psychiatrist has to answer this important question: 'Why is this person suffering from depression?' If they can discover a specific event that the depression may be a reaction to, or has been precipitated by, then the depression is known as a reactive or neurotic depression. If no apparent reason can be found and the depression has simply arrived, then the person may be suffering from an endogenous depression, 'endogenous' being derived from the Greek word for 'arising from within'. This type of depression is thought to be caused by a change in the chemical balance of the brain or the hormone balance in our bodies. It is also known as psychotic depression, as a person can lose touch with reality during this depression and experience hallucinations, have delusional ideas or hear voices.

These two broad classifications of depression are only 'approximate' guides as there are some people who experience different forms of depression. Melanie has been through two periods of depression. In the first the depression and the attempted suicide were caused by the feelings she had about herself after being emotionally blackmailed by someone she had trusted. She describes that depressive experience as, 'Absolute darkness, sheer, blind panic.' Melanie visited her GP who offered her little help. Grudgingly she went to see a psychotherapist which she did not feel did her any good. Over a period of time, with the help of some friends, one of whom was a counsellor, Melanie came out of the darkness. This had clearly been a reactive depression.

Two years later Melanie was depressed again but she knew it felt like a very different type of depression: 'I experienced extreme lethargy, lost all ability to concentrate, felt listless and unable to motivate myself.' There was not the same sense of despair, but it was still an unpleasant experience that brought back fears as to whether or not she would ever get better. Her doctor diagnosed an endogenous depression caused by a chemical imbalance and she returned to her normal self after a course of antidepressants. Melanie had been through first a reactive type of depression and secondly an endogenous depression; she knew they felt like very different types of depression, even though there were some common features.

## 1. Reactive depression

Tracey could have been in *Eastenders*. She came from the same close-knit family background and her life revolved round the 'local', blokes and nightclubbing. She possessed good looks, an attractive figure and dressed in the latest fashions. Added to this was a vivacious personality which went down well in her job as a hairdresser. Everything looked good and she had all her plans made for the future, like her twenty-first birthday party. Then Simon told her it was over. Tracey plunged into depression. The family rallied round, the customers were understanding, but Tracey found herself utterly alone and didn't want to live. She tried to commit suicide by taking an overdose of paracetamol, and when this did not succeed Tracey became a voluntary patient in a psychiatric hospital. When I met her here, Tracey seemed like a porcelain doll, very beautiful and immensely fragile. She wrote me a poem called 'Sadness' expressing how she felt:

> Have you ever felt so sad,
> That you don't know what to say,
> Have you ever felt so sad,
> That you wish your life away.
>
> Have you ever tried to explain,
> Then found you just can't speak,
> Have you ever lived with pain,
> When each minute lasts a week?
>
> Well, I have felt that sorrow,
> And there's nothing I can do,
> Each night I curse tomorrow,
> As I curse my love for you.

Over the weeks Tracey started cutting the other patients' hair and as she felt she was useful became more able to talk about what had led up to her suicide attempt. Tracey had felt rejected by Simon at the very core of her being. It was as if the very fabric of life had been ripped from her. All her life Tracey had been the centre of attention. As a child her big blue eyes, blonde curls and mischievous grin had got her own way. As a teenager she had the boys queuing up to go out with her, something that she had really enjoyed. Life had seemed like a big party, until now. The loss of Simon had made Tracey discover a whole range of feelings about herself that she had never realised before. After a month Tracey felt able to leave hospital, aware that she was not the same person as before. She had suffered from a reactive or neurotic depression.

The causes of this type of depression may be fairly obvious, such as redundancy or divorce, in which case the depression is a reaction to these circumstances. There may be other causes of the depression which are not so easy to isolate. If as a helper we find ourselves listening to someone like Tracey or Rachel who are showing clear signs of depression (see Chapter 1) then they really need to see their GP. If they think it is necessary they will refer the person to a psychiatrist or they may feel that a course of antidepressant drugs is necessary. Much as some GPs would love to, they rarely have the time to go in detail into a person's life to explore the real cause of the depression. They are not in a position to make a long-term commitment to work through the issues that may be causing the depression. It is here that a supportive family, friend, pastor or counsellor can be of great help.

*Treating reactive depression*

Befriending, listening, love and care, greatly help people who are depressed. More will be said about this in Chapter 7. However, while telling somebody else how they feel is help enough, for some people, there are several forms of treatment that only a doctor is able to give to a depressed person. A doctor is able to reassure the person that they do not have some dreadful disease or that they are not going mad.

When a person is depressed, they often experience a whole range of minor symptoms related to anxiety. They often go to the doctor because of these symptoms rather than because they realise they are depressed. The appropriate treatment however is not a mild tranquilliser but an anti-depressant drug. These reduce the symptoms of depression, with some drugs working better with some people than others. Helen saw her GP who gave her one course of drugs which had little effect but on changing the drug, Helen made a rapid recovery.

Quite a number of psychiatrists see the use of drugs in reactive depression as having a low priority. The aim—whatever the treatment—is to enable the person to cope with the painful process of exploring who they are and what has made them the way they are. This is best done with someone who has had experience of counselling others. There may be some side effects with the drugs, such as blurred vision, a dry mouth and drowsiness, and it has been found helpful to keep people on anti-depressants for up to six months after they are feeling better as this has been shown to prevent relapses in many cases. Care must be taken, however, as an overdose on a small number of certain antidepressant drugs can be fatal.

## 2. Endogenous depression

Alan adjusted quickly to his new life as an engineering student. He soon made friends on his course and in the Christian Union. The work kept him busy but still left him enough time to enjoy life as a student with the freedom from home, the late night conversations, the Film Club and the odd game of hockey. Alan coped with the work, passed his first-year and second-year exams. During the third year, he found he was becoming increasingly critical of other people and found himself spending more and more time in his room. He just didn't seem to be able to concentrate. Worship, which he had always enjoyed, seemed remote and he felt that God did not care. Alan thought that if he worked harder matters would improve. They did not. He tried being more disciplined in spending more time in prayer but that had no effect either. By the second term he had given up working and spent most of his time alone in his room or wandering round the city. He saw few friends and had nothing to say when he did meet them. A darkness had engulfed him that blotted out everything. One day he found himself down by the docks, thinking, 'Why don't I just throw myself in? That will be an answer to everything; I won't have to worry about work then.' At this point he realised that he had a problem and went to the doctor for help. Alan was suffering from endogenous or psychotic depression.

*Treating endogenous depression*

The treatment offered to people with depression varies. However other than psychotherapy it has been found that three particular forms of treatment are more likely to have good effect in cases of severe depression. These are the use of antidepressants, lithium and a much older method, electro-convulsive therapy (ECT) also known as 'shock' treatment.

The biggest problem with antidepressant drugs is getting a depressed person to take them. This task is made more difficult by the fact that they often take up to two weeks before any effect is noticed by the person taking them.

Lithium carbonate, a naturally occurring salt, is used particularly in manic-depression as it has been found that it often reduces the length and severity of the swings in mood and the frequency of depression. There are side effects and regular blood checks are important. It is not a quick-acting treatment and may be used in conjunction with ECT.

Forty years ago ECT was the only method available for treating very depressed and psychotic patients. As a consequence it was probably over used and not always used wisely. Nowadays a person is given an anaesthetic and a muscle relaxant, then an electrical charge is passed through the brain which results in the body having a convulsion, similar to an epileptic fit. The person does not suffer any after effects other than a bit of a headache and a slight loss of memory concerning the last couple of hours. It has been discovered that not everyone benefits from ECT but that for many its use halts their depression and the suicidal tendencies that often accompany this form of depression.

Some Christians oppose the use of ECT as we do not know exactly what happens and how it brings about this change. All that can be said is that since its use the number of deaths by suicide of depressed people has fallen. Anne was a church youth leader, who suffered from manic depression, which seemed to come back in a cycle each year. When it happened she would become very aggressive and paranoid, resulting in a short stay in a psychiatric hospital. Here she was given ECT and every time she made a rapid recovery. While ECT can be of great help to some people it does not prevent the depression recurring. Other Christians oppose the use of drugs, but here is one depressed person's response.

> So often such a course of continual medication is seen as a Christian defeat...I ask, why? Why a defeat, when it is not defeat to take pills to control angina...for me, spiritual renewal came after the lifting of the cloud (through drugs)...not through claiming healing, or my determining to reorganise my life, or through some Spirit-given insight into the truth of God.... It came simply through the cry of utter des-

peration, which recognised God's absolute sovereignty, and my own abject poverty, and the deep, unarticulated, vaguely-formed, but real, knowledge that somehow, for no virtue in me, I was important to God because he loved me — that he cared, even for the emotional, depressed wreck of a Christian prostrate before him.[3]

Because there are times when people suffering from this form of depression may lose touch with reality, they can become a possible danger to themselves or to others and may need to be admitted to a psychiatric hospital, sometimes against their will. There is provision under the 1983 Mental Health Act for compulsory admission to hospital, though there are safeguards to prevent this from being abused. It is important that regular visits from family, church members and the pastor makes sure the person is not forgotten. It is even more encouraging when one comes across members of staff who are also Christians.

## 3. Manic depression

One form of depression is manic depressive psychosis. In this illness the person swings from great excitement (mania), to profound depression with a clear loss of touch with reality. Psychotic symptoms emerge. One such symptom is delusions. These are false, unshakable beliefs which are not in keeping with the culture of the person. They often believe themselves to be somebody of great importance, such as Napoleon, and can be of a religious nature, like being the Messiah or a prophet. One patient I worked with did not believe himself to be Christ, but one of his special disciples who had a special code by which he could speak to the Lord.

Uni-polar depression is very similar to manic depression, except that there is no upward, manic swing. The person's thinking will be very negative, for example, 'I am the most awful sinner in the world. God will never forgive me for having such dreadful thoughts. All I deserve is to rot in hell.' Often these delusions can be linked to paranoia where the person fears everybody and believes that people are conspiring against them in order to get their special powers or their secrets. One young man felt that everybody was out to attack him and so began to carry a sword for his own protection. When the police tried to arrest him for brandishing this in the high street he was even more convinced that he was right after all!

Other symptoms are hearing or seeing things that are not there. Often the person believes they have either received a message from God or had visions of God, the devil or hell. There can also be a distinct change in the person's character and behaviour while on the way up, in a manic phase or on the way down, in a depressive phase. The person's expression of their sexuality may change. They may talk about sex more, make more frequent sexual demands within marriage or become promiscuous. There can be an increased consumption of alcohol as well as aggression and potential violence.

Other symptoms include poor appetite, disrupted sleep patterns and exhaustion.

As you would expect in the course of such an illness the person has little understanding of what is going on. Their insight into their situation is impaired for much of the time.

## 4. Post-natal depression

This is a common form of depression, affecting many women. It illustrates how complex depression is as it bridges both reactive and endogenous types of depression.

Helen is in her early thirties with two young children. Happily married, Helen is a 'down to earth' Londoner. Since Kerry, her first child's birth, Helen has been depressed. At first she thought it would pass—it was the 'blues' that all mums go through. Then she put it down to her hormones, then to her weight which she had put on during pregnancy and never lost. Still she found herself despairing, drowning in an endless cycle of events. She was tired by sleepless nights and infuriated by the constant demands of this baby that never gave her a minute's peace. Simple tasks like making a meal, washing breakfast dishes or housework took hours. Her husband was very understanding but found himself helpless and hurt by the explosions of anger and tears. Helen stopped going out of the house and even when friends called would sit in a chair and stare into space. Within herself Helen felt she was neglecting the kids and destroying the family. 'Why don't I end it all?' she thought, 'I'm a useless wife, we don't even have sex anymore, my husband is probably repulsed by my body anyway. As for the children, look at the way I scream and shout at them for the least little thing. How can they grow up normal with a mother like me?'

It is common after the birth of a child for mothers to experience the 'baby blues'—a state of being emotionally upset, frightened, confused and tearful. When you think what that mum has just been through: pain caused by stitches, breast feeding, sheer exhaustion, hormonal imbalances, and the process of adjustment to the new baby, it is not surprising that one in two mums experience this.

Helen, however, had something more severe than this. Helen is one of the one in ten mothers who suffer from post-natal depression. Sometimes this is a continuation of the 'baby blues' but it can just happen any time up to about three months after giving birth. The reasons mothers get depressed are both physical and psychological.

A small number of mothers, about two or three in a thousand develop some psychotic symptoms such as hearing voices or seeing hallucinations as part of their depression. One mother became convinced that her baby had died at birth and that she had been given another one that was not really hers. Another mother believed that there had been a nuclear war and that all her feelings of excitement, her inability to sleep or eat were due to the effects of the radiation. When a person becomes divorced from reality they obviously need hospital treatment and there is possibly some question of risk to the baby or other members of the family. Frightening as this form of depression is it can be well treated, though of all the forms of post-natal depression it is the one most likely to recur in future pregnancies.

*Treating post-natal depression*

One of the consequences of having a child is the isolation that it brings. Some women have given up work, others are away from their family, and most find it difficult to get around and see the friends they once did. If they then begin to suffer from depression it can go unnoticed unless there are people around who know what to look for. It is important that family or friends are able to recognise the features that indicate depression.

One helpful person is the health visitor. During pregnancy a health visitor will have been to see the mum-to-be and after the baby is born will be back to see the mum and new baby. Their experience is vital in alerting them to the fact that a mum might be depressed and for some mums with family and friends far away, they are the only person they feel they can talk to.

Talking in a group or over the phone to someone who has been through a similar experience is profoundly helpful. It makes one feel that despite everything we are normal after all and that there can be an end to the blackness, that the fog will lift. Such groups can be contacted through:

The Association for Post-natal Illness, 7 Gowan Avenue, Fulham, London SW6 6RH.

Meet-a-Mum Association (MAMA), 5 Westbury Gardens, Luton, LU2 7DW.

The National Childbirth Trust, 9 Queensborough Terrace, London W2.

Otherwise the treatment for post-natal depression is the same as other forms of depression.

## Further reading

David Stafford-Clark and Andrew Smith, *Psychiatry for Students*, Sixth Edition (George Allen & Unwin: London, 1983).
Nicholas Rose, Ed, *Essential Psychiatry* (Blackwell Scientific Publications: Oxford, 1988).

# 5

## *The Christian and Depression*

While on a hospital chaplain's course at a psychiatric hospital I remember asking a consultant psychiatrist if Christians got depressed. The question reflected my genuine belief that because salvation meets the deepest human needs, somehow that prevented us from facing such problems. Her reply was, 'Of course: they're human beings aren't they?' The combination of our humanity and the spiritual reality of being a Christian can lead to some confusion. Two areas that cause difficulty for Christians are the demonic and spiritual depression.

### The demonic

Some psychiatrists are not very comfortable talking about demons. Such a suggestion is seen as: a return to medieval superstition; a naive understanding of what is happening to a person; a way of sensationalising a more mundane problem; or a denial that there is a problem at all. It is a complicated subject that cannot be written off quite as easily as some in the medical world would suggest. Even Christians are not very comfortable talking about the demonic and there tends to be two polarised responses. Some Christians see demons as the cause of anything, including depression, that they have no neat answer for. Others see it as a spiritual term for the dark side of our human nature where the problem is psychological, not spiritual. There needs to be a recognition of both our psychological and spiritual make-up, and if we get involved in this area four factors need to be borne in mind.

1. People who have any kind of involvement in occult activities leave themselves vulnerable to demonic influence and often experience depression as part of a whole list of unpleasant consequences. Dr Stuart Checkley, a consultant psychiatrist at the Maudsley Hospital sees depression as a major feature of occult activity. Similarly, Dr Russell Blacker, a consultant psychiatrist at The Royal Cornwall Hospital, Truro, who specialises in depression has said, 'I have seen a handful of cases where there is some malign spiritual influence at work.'

2. It is my understanding that the Bible supports the view that the devil is a real being, that demons are to be found today and that while Christians cannot be possessed by evil spirits there are times when they have a foothold in our lives and can oppress and depress us (Eph 4:27). The Bible makes it clear to Christians that they are in a spiritual battle (Eph 6:12). One of the things we have to contend with is our old nature, as Paul clearly

illustrates: 'When I want to do good, evil is right there with me...waging war.... What a wretched man I am' (Rom 7:21–24). Dr Lloyd-Jones suggests, 'The devil takes hold of self and uses it in order to depress us.' If by our nature we are prone to depression, then the devil will do the utmost to discourage us. That does not mean that the cause of the depression is demonic, simply that we should be aware of the spiritual forces which may be at work.

3. Reference to a 'demon', 'possession' or 'dark forces' can be a way of avoiding the problems we face in those areas of ourselves that we are unhappy with. Mary was a young mother in her early twenties who struck me as intelligent and perceptive. Formerly she had been a very active church worker. In her depression she believed that she was dying. She was like a leaf just about to fall from a tree to be swept away for ever. Mary said that the reason for this was that she had committed the 'unforgivable sin' and surrendered her life to the devil. She felt that her life was under a heavy shadow, that she was surrounded by an incredibly debilitating presence. When asked to describe her 'devil' she said that it was religious, powerful, it never let up and was destructive. 'I love him, I want him to love me,' was Mary's response when she was asked why she didn't get rid of her 'devil'. Some time later, as part of a therapeutic group, we were acting out a scene from her life where I played her father, who had been both a very 'religious' man and an extremely strict disciplinarian. She slapped me hard across the cheek and cried, 'I only wanted you to love me

as a naughty little girl'. Mary's 'devil' was tied up with experiences and feelings in her past and in the present about her father.

4. A woman who had suffered with post-natal depression came to see me. Her depression had gone on for over two years. As I listened it became clear that the root of the problem went back to her anger at being rejected by her mother as a child. As part of a counselling process we imagined a situation with Jesus reaching out to accept her. She later told me that during this time Jesus had 'ripped' something away from her and that she felt different. As we explored this further it seemed that Jesus had removed a demon from her. From that day she has not suffered from depression for a single day, when it had been her everyday experience for years. Her husband has said he still can't get over how happy she is. For months both of them were expecting everything to come crashing down and go back to the old depressed ways. That has still not happened. Though there are areas that she has discovered that she has to work on, such as forgiving her mother, she is able to do so with the energy that depression robbed her of. It is possible, though I would suggest relatively rare, for depression to be caused by a demon. As Dr Checkley says, 'Sometimes you cannot explain it in psychiatric ways.'

These matters, because of their complexity, should really be dealt with by doctors and pastors who have an understanding of both psychiatric illness and the demonic.

## Spiritual depression

Some Christians talk about spiritual depression. Just as depression robs a person of the ability to enjoy life, so spiritual depression robs a Christian of the ability to enjoy their Christian life. Dr Lloyd-Jones suggests at least twenty ways in which we can be affected by spiritual depression, sometimes bringing it on ourselves. This is an experience that many Christians face in the course of life and they need help and encouragement. Real discernment is needed to make sure that Christians are not spiritualising a genuine experience of depression. Spiritual depression should not be confused with depression.

If we suffer from any kind of depression, no matter how brief, it will affect our spiritual life. You only have to read the Psalms to discover that depression was an experience faced by David and others. The 'Joy of the Lord is my strength' became 'Tears have been my food day and night'. Jeremiah wrote a whole book of mournful lamentations. God may seem remote, harsh, angry, uncaring and uninvolved. The Bible becomes a book of empty or meaningless words. The Church and its services seem an empty ritual and a mouthing of words that we do not believe at that moment. Every sermon leaves us condemned and accused. We feel isolated, deserted and alone and then guilty because we know it should be different. But this is not spiritual depression.

Peter came to see me because things were not going well spiritually. We talked about home and family, work, marriage and how he felt about himself. It became clear that the cause of his spiritual depression was that he was setting unrealistic goals for himself as a Christian. When Peter realised that he did not have to earn God's love or approval by what he did, his whole spiritual life began to grow again as he moved out of this state of spiritual depression. Perhaps the biggest cause of spiritual depression is plain, old-fashioned sin (1 Jn 1:8–9). We need to deal with that sin but should also take note of the attitude shown by David, 'Forgive my hidden faults. Keep your servant from wilful sin' (Ps 19:12–13).

Other Christians talk about 'the dark night of the soul'. This is part of a mystical expression of the Christian faith which talks of abandonment, detachment and darkness. While this spiritual experience has some features similar to depression, it is quite different. A young man who had been unemployed for eighteen months told me that during this time he felt he had gone through a 'dark night of the soul'. It would have been more accurate to say that he had experienced depression. He obviously found it easier to acknowledge a spiritual cause of his turmoil rather than any other. Most pastors have enough experience to distinguish between depression and spiritual depression, but if they are in any doubt they should always suggest a person sees their doctor.

## Further reading

Russ Parker, *The Occult: Deliverance from Evil* (IVP: Leicester, 1989).

Andrew Sims, 'Demon Possession: Medical Perspectives in a Western Culture,' *Medicine and the Bible*, Bernard Palmer (Ed.) (Paternoster Press: Exeter, 1986).

# 6

## *Depression and Suicide*

During the writing of this book, one of the members of my church committed suicide. Hilary was a teacher who was finding the demands of the job incredibly tough. Along with some other major changes in her life and moving house it all became too much for her. As Hilary talked with me she focused on her job as being the source of the problem. I suggested she go and see a lady who was both a good listener and a deputy head. Hilary did this, but the next Sunday said she still did not feel any better and was obviously depressed. I felt she ought to go and see her doctor as soon as possible (Monday) and arranged to see her for some counselling on the Wednesday. On the Tuesday, Hilary committed suicide.

I felt a complete failure, that I had let Hilary and her husband down. I thought, 'How can I write a book on depression when I let something like this happen?' Over a period of time I came to see that in reality I could not have given Hilary any more help than I had. I no longer feel so guilty, but I still feel pain about those events, and it has increased my desire to try to help others in such pain. It also raised a number of questions.

## 1. Why do Christians commit suicide?

Christians have fears, hopes, anxieties and despairs like the rest of the human race. Depression, in particular, robs us of rational thinking. Of all the people who commit suicide over fifty per cent have been diagnosed as clinically depressed. Another particularly vulnerable group are the bereaved. When a loved one has died there is an almost overwhelming desire to be with them, even for many Christians. At that point, suicide seems a natural thing to do. Christians are not immune from committing suicide. In fact in a strange kind of a way, because Christians believe in life after death, the prospect of death itself loses some of its terror (1 Cor 15:55) and may while they are depressed make suicide seem less awful than it is. A mother who killed herself, leaving a young family behind, said in a letter that she did not expect them to understand why she was doing this but the fact that one day she would see them in heaven was a comfort to her.

There are seven references to suicide in the Bible (Abimelech—Judg 9:54; Samson—Judg 16:30; Saul and his armour bearer—1 Sam 31:4–5; Ahitophel—2 Sam 17:23; Zimri—1 Kings 16:18; and Judas—Mt 27:5). In all but Samson's case these people were clearly outside the will of God. The taking of one's life is still falling short of what

God intends for our lives but the fact that Christians do contemplate suicide while depressed shows the seriousness of the matter.

## 2. What about attempted or parasuicide?

In an effort to call attention to their pain and their predicament some people who do not intend to kill themselves make some attempt, such as taking an overdose of tablets or slashing their wrists. They do so because the mention of the word suicide has everyone sitting on the edge of their seats or rushing around in panic. It certainly brings a great deal of attention to the person concerned. I was asked to go and see a student who had locked himself in his room after being seen brandishing a knife and talking about suicide. In fact he had merely scratched his wrists with a plastic knife. As we talked it emerged that he felt worthless because his girlfriend had broken off their relationship.

Most acts of attempted suicide are a very angry cry for help, often meant for someone close to hear, such as a partner or a parent. It is most likely to happen when there is some threat to a relationship, ie a husband threatening to commit suicide if his wife leaves him for someone else.

Any suicide threat must be taken seriously, as eighty per cent of people who kill themselves have given notice of their intent. What should you do if someone threatens this? Firstly, don't panic. Your increased anxiety might confuse the situation. Secondly, try and ascertain how serious the threat is. If you think there is a real risk, don't leave the person on their own. If they are under the influence of alcohol they may think quite differently when sober. Thirdly, tell someone such as a minister, doctor, or social worker who is involved with that person. Fourthly, talk to the person and ask what the pain is all about. Simply having someone who listens can restore the perspective of the situation.

There is also a difficulty with antidepressant drugs: when people are very depressed they often do not have the energy to commit suicide, but as the drug takes effect and gives them more energy they are capable of it. While this should not halt the prescription of antidepressants it should be noted by those who care if the person has given any indication that they might attempt suicide.

## Further reading

Gary Collins, 'Why Would a Good Christian Ever Attempt Suicide?', *Can You Trust Counselling* (IVP: Leicester, 1988).
G. Lloyd Carr, *After the Storm. Hope in the Wake of Suicide* (IVP: Leicester, 1990).

# 7

## *Helping the Depressed*

The challenge of caring for depressed people is daunting, but one we are called to do if we are to 'Carry each others burdens' (Gal 6:2).[4] But who does the caring? Depression is something not everyone can cope with, but if we have any desire to care for others we will end up helping people who are depressed as there is so much depression about. It is very easy in a church context to talk about loving one another but somewhere this needs to find practical expression.

Not everyone is able to care for the depressed. Some people will not have the desire, ability, time or energy to care. Ian was looking forward to retirement but when it happened he became depressed. This is natural enough as there are inevitable feelings of loss at this time. His wife Jill could not cope with the depression at all. She kept going back over how in the tough times in her life she had to get on with life and cope: 'If only he would pull himself together and stop being so selfish, moping around all day,' she would say. In other areas Jill was a good carer but in this she found great difficulty.

I sent a questionnaire to a number of depressed people. One question asked was, 'What was the worst piece of advice given?' The answers fall into three categories and were mainly given by GPs, pastors and home-group leaders.

The first category dismisses the problem. One student was told she was a 'silly girl', a young man was informed, 'When you have a family you'll find there are more important things to bother about and the problem will disappear', and a middle-aged woman was told, 'Do you want to go to the funny farm?'

The second category blames the person. 'You shouldn't have joined that church in the first place.' 'What did you expect after doing what you did?' Both answers increased the sense of blame and guilt.

The third category indicates an unrealistic response. One girl was told by a friend that the cause was obviously demonic. When someone told their home-group leader about feeling depressed, he said he would go away and ask the Lord what he was saying in the situation. The home-group leader never referred to it again. Another church member shared their problem with a church leader, who prayed for them to be healed. Months went by, and when the person asked their leader why they had not done anything else they were told it would have been a lack of faith.

## Who can care?

A depressed person often thinks, 'Nobody cares.' In fact there are individuals and groups of people who can provide a safety-net that will try and catch the falling person from the tight-rope walk that depression has become.

### 1. The family

Some husbands or wives are towers of strength who during their partner's depression become housekeeper, nursemaid, cook, chauffer as well as holding down a full-time job. Others do not have the resources to cope with such a crisis and pretend that there is not really a problem. Help comes by being honest and bringing the problem into the open. Even sharing one's fears can bring to light the extent of the depression, and the family can at least make sense of what is happening. Families can hold onto the fact that for most people there will be an end to the depression. There is hope, even if the person cannot see it at the time.

### 2. Friends

Friends are worth their weight in gold because they can see things in us we cannot see ourselves and will love us just as much when we are depressed. When Amy told a friend she was feeling a bit down, a few days later Joan turned up out of the blue with a card and a present to show that she cared. More practically she went into the kitchen and started to wash up the dishes. The presence of friends is another source of hope. A friend can go with the person to the doctor to help their friend ask for help or say they are not happy about the treatment.

## 3. Doctors

They see many depressed people. One mother went to her doctor about 'piles' and he gently asked her how she was getting on with the new baby. She felt able to say that the real problem was that she was feeling so tired and it all seemed so hopeless. However, the time pressures on doctors are immense and they do not always have the time to listen in depth.

## 4. The church

Every church should have someone or some group who has a specific role in caring for those in need. Many Christians still have problem recognising and dealing with emotional or psychological problems. There can be a dangerous 'narrowness' that believes that personal faith in Christ answers everyone's problems. Churches talk about caring, but they tend to be very busy places and it is easy for an individuals' needs to get swamped by all the activity.

We need to regain the ability seen in Jesus to spot and care for the needy individual in a crowd (Mk 5:26–34; Lk 19:2–10). At its best the church can be a therapeutic community that restores and repairs those in need through its worship, ministry and people.

## 5. Hospitals

Sadly there is still stigma attached to mental illness and a stay at a psychiatric hospital. As many of them were built in Victorian days their appearance can be quite forbidding. Their exterior belies the wealth of care within and increasingly that care is being made available in the community. Families are often relieved that there is a 'safe place' for someone they love to be looked after for a short period of time.

## 6. Self-help groups

A little has been said about these in Chapter 4. One such group, Islington Women and Mental Health Project, published a booklet *Women and Depression* which looks at the subject from a woman's perspective. They can be contacted at Caxton House, 129 St John's Way, London N19 3RU. Other helpful addresses are:

Depressives Associated, PO Box 5, Castle Town, Portland, Dorset DT5 1BQ.

MIND (National Association for Mental Health), 22 Harley Street, London W1N 2ED. (Mind often has local branches.)

The Fellowship of Depressives Anonymous, 36 Chestnut Avenue, Beverly, North Humberside, HU17 9QU.

## How can I care?

There are a number of simple steps that enable us to be better carers with depressed people. The most valuable help is practical and on-going and, is best done in a low-key way. This is the sort of help that a home-group could provide.

### 1. Understanding the problem

Any carer will need to have some understanding of depression. It is for that reason that this book has been written. Of itself it will not make you an expert carer, but it provides an overall framework which can help you to help others. 'The heart of the discerning acquires knowledge; the ears of the wise seek it out' (Prov 18:15).

### 2. Understanding ourselves

Here are a number of questions we need to ask ourselves if we want to get involved. It is helpful to get a good friend to help. Composing the answers might well be an education and a shock!

(i) How good are we at listening? In conversation do we find it difficult to stop talking or jumping in with answers?

(ii) How do we cope with strong feelings? When was the last time we were angry and what did that feel like? How well did we cope with ourselves then?

(iii) Do we possess patience and persistence? Are we going to be around for some time?

(iv) How do we cope when we hear something that shocks us?

(v) Have we been depressed? Can we be objective in helping another person whose depression may be very different? Can we avoid the temptation of telling our experience and answers?

(vi) What are our motives? A friend or pastor will be helpful in unravelling what these might be. For example, we all like to be appreciated and needed. Sometimes people latch onto others to meet their own needs rather than really being able to help.

## 3. Setting limits

Jesus had a number of very clear priorities, which meant he chose to limit the times and the places he was available to care (Mk 1:35–39). Being available to help does not mean you have to be 'on-call' twenty-four hours a day. A quick chat, a regular phone-call, the willingness to simply be there with someone in their silence can be of great value. To have someone who will drop in two or three times a week, to do some shopping, cooking a meal or baby-sitting is a practical way of showing the depressed person that they are of value and not forgotten. Get others to help so that it does not always land on your doorstep.

This stops the problem of the person becoming too dependent on you. The better we know ourselves the better we are able to say 'I can help so far but no further'. Once someone is involved in helping a depressed person it is easy to be drawn in out of their depth. Sometimes there are feelings of failure, of letting someone down, or of there being no one else available. However more harm can be done by not facing these issues rather than avoiding them. It is therefore good to be clear about the limits of time, energy and care that is available at the start of the helping process.

## 4. Facing the problem

No person can really benefit from help unless they are prepared to admit there is a problem. Even though it may be obvious to others, until that person realises they are depressed any care will have a limited effect. Sometimes our first task is to make the person aware that there is a problem in as gentle a way as possible. All of us find failure difficult to handle, and depression feels like failure, like letting oneself and God down. It is a painful moment when somebody draws attention to depression, unless with it is also communicated a similar concern and care.

## 5. Establishing trust

In order for any help to be given the person needs to feel they can trust us. Trust is a fragile thing that is slowly built and easily destroyed. If the person thinks we will be critical or dismissive then they may not tell us what it is they are feeling, or not give us the full picture until they feel able to trust us sufficiently. After all, most people test the water temperature before diving in. Many depressed people say that when they tell someone how they feel they are not believed, and this is a real problem in establishing trust.

A common starting point is, 'I am having trouble with my quiet times.' If we are honest we all have trouble with our quiet times; but we must be careful how we respond. If we were to say, 'Well it is really just a matter of discipline. What you need is an alarm clock. I am sure if you try harder...', the person will be thinking, 'Is he really hearing what it is I am saying?' 'He doesn't seem to be very understanding,' 'It is quite obvious that he is far too busy.' What we feel and think when a person shares with us is usually communicated by our words, tone of voice and facial expression. All these factors help to establish trust. The easiest way to destroy trust is to betray the confidence of someone. Anything that is told to us should be treated as confidential unless we have obtained permission to share the situation with someone else.

## 6. Listen

When we have a problem the person we seek out to talk to is someone who is a good listener. We live in a world where there are many words, much noise and little listening. It is increasingly common when I call round on people to have to hold a conversation while the TV drones on. The result is that we are used to noise and quite capable of ignoring it, thus making listening a thing we do less and less.

Dr Paul Tournier has made this observation:

> It is impossible to over-emphasise the immense need human beings have to be listened to...in most conversations, although there is a good deal of talk, there is

75

not real listening; such conversations are no more than a dialogue of the deaf.[5]

The book of Proverbs is scathing of those who 'Delight in airing their own opinion' (18:2) and 'who answer(s) before listening' (18:13). While working for a church when I was training for the ministry I remember being asked to visit a home where somebody had died. This was the first time I had ever had to do such a thing and I had little idea what to do. It was painful to sit there because in the face of death it seemed a bit trite to trot out the biblical verses that talk of the 'sting' of death being removed. So out of ignorance rather than wisdom I sat and let the woman share her pain and loss. I now realise that I had done the best thing possible, listen. Rather than avoid my own pain and confusion by quoting Bible verses I had sat and shared someone else's pain. Interestingly, this lady has said many times how helpful that visit was. At least Job's friends got it right by sitting and listening for a week, even if their subsequent arguments were of little help (Job 2:11–13).

Listening is hard work, requiring concentration and practice. We have to pick up the clues that are given to us. Rarely will someone tell us immediately what their pressing problem is. Think about yourself for a moment. How easily do you ask for help? It is something most of us are not very good at. To ask for help often seems like admitting we have failed. To ask for help means making oneself vulnerable and takes the risk of rejection. Each person is an individual, with an individual story, and each person needs to be listened to.

As a person talks with us and we listen, one way of helping is to clarify what it is the person is actually saying. Sometimes we know that something is wrong, we feel unhappy but can't quite put exact words or feelings to it. A friend who listens is able to clarify our situation by giving us time, letting us meander and explore an area that concerns us. The very act of putting into words what it is we have been thinking and feelings helps us to see the situation in a clearer way. The help of a suitable question can make the situation clearer for both people. Sometimes we are told long, involved stories where we need to make sure we have heard what it is the person has said. Questions like, 'Are you saying…' 'I wonder how you feel at the moment…', help to ensure that we have heard what is being said and what our friend feels about that. Try to avoid asking questions like, 'Why did you…' as they can feel very threatening. If the person knew, they would not be talking about it now. As you listen, put together a history of the person, think about what has not been said, observe what they are like and what they indicate by their tone of voice and eye-contact.

If they have not yet seen their GP encourage them to do so as there is still a 'gut' fear of any emotional or mental illness. Often the fear is of ending up in a 'loony bin'. This can be helpfully talked through and any fears allayed.

How depressed is this person? Because of their

very problem a depressed person is not likely to have great insight into why they are depressed or have a particularly high opinion of themselves. It may be that they are too depressed for us to do more than provide support until the antidepressant drugs take effect which can be up to three weeks from first taking them.

## 7. *Setting goals*

Suggest to the depressed person that they make a list of all the things that they enjoy but have stopped doing since they have become depressed. Get them to give a score out of seven as to how hard it would be to start doing each activity again. Starting with the easiest task, sit down and plan in detail how and when they can start doing that activity again.

Encourage the person to set simple, attainable goals for themselves. If we end up suggesting the goals, which may initially happen, we may be too demanding. These goals could include eating properly, getting some exercise, being more active or even a simple job in the church. This is part of a vital process of getting the person to take responsibility for their own lives.

> I found it useful to plan each day the previous evening so that when I awoke panic stricken, I had my day worked out...I found it easier at first to do things for others rather than for myself, e.g. take the kids to the park...I also found it easier to do things where I had a set task to perform...I am attempting to rebuild my life through activities rather than by sitting back and

waiting to get better.... It does help to take the kids to the park or whatever because it makes them happy and increases your own self-esteem. You cannot be totally evil if you can make someone a bit happier.[6]

## 8. Encourage positive thinking

When someone thinks negatively try to reason with them and don't agree just to make life easier. Try and put their negative comment in a positive way. For example:

NEGATIVE COMMENT: 'Don't waste your time on me';
UNHELPFUL RESPONSE: 'Don't bother anyone with your so called problem. You'll probably feel better tomorrow';
POSITIVE RESPONSE: 'I want to help because I care. Let's work out where we can get the best help.'

One husband was convinced he was going to fail all his exams. His wife firmly but consistently said that in view of the course marks he had achieved and the amount of revision he had done he was likely to pass the exam. Stating the truth calmly can sometimes help the depressed person to see things in a different light.

## 9. Support the rest of the family

Depression affects families. The partner of the depressed person lives with depression every day and often feels helpless or guilty about not coping or not being able to do more. For these reasons when help is being given they often do not ask for any.

79

This is partly because they are not 'ill' in the same way their partner is and they feel guilty about making demands on already busy people. If there are any children it is helpful to keep an eye on them as they may need that little bit more understanding. A teenager was having trouble settling at a new school and at a youth meeting began to talk about it. It turned out that her mother had been depressed for several years and while this was not the only problem, part of Angela's rebellion was to do with never getting the attention from her mother that she wanted.

## 10. Prayer, the Bible and worship

Prayer is something we can do that a depressed person is often not able to do for themselves. One minister's future seemed bleak when he discovered he suffered from manic depression. He was prayed for very specifically—with dramatic results. The extremes of his depression became less severe to the extent that he could continue working normally for most of the time. Sometimes the prayer goes 'unanswered' and the depression remains the same. Even though we feel abandoned by God, he is still there.

Depression does not always help concentration, and daily reading, if that was a practice before, becomes difficult. However, because the Bible is the inspired word of God, the Holy Spirit is able to minister truth that reaches into and speaks to the very depths of a person. The Bible encourages us to think positively and deal with our learned helplessness, anger, guilt and despair. It shows us God's perspective on our situation. Here is a list of scriptures that depressed people have found to be helpful:

Psalm 23; 42; 43:5; 138:8; 139; 143; Isaiah 28:23–29; 42:3; 43:1–3; 54:10; 57:15; Jeremiah 29:11–14; 31:3–4; Lamentations 3:22; Micah 7:7–9; Matthew 11:28; Romans 8:1; 8:28–39; 1 Corinthians 10:13; 2 Corinthians 1:3–4; 4:17–18; Philippians 1:6; 4:8; James 1:2–4.

Encourage the depressed person to remain part of a worshipping community. This is not always easy as the depressed person may feel that everyone is smiling and happy except them. They might be anxious about crying in church and not want the fuss that could give rise to. They may not know what to say when someone comes up and asks how they are. A practical step is to go with the friend and act as a 'minder'.

Often depressed people need to be reminded that they are not the only people in the world and this so naturally happens when we worship. Our focus is on God who truly knows us and truly loves us. A vital part of any church's worship is the celebration of communion and for some depressed people this is a truly healing act. As we share in the Lord's Supper, we receive bread and wine. These are tangible, physical signs that God has not abandoned us and has come to be with us.

# Further reading

Duncan Buchanan, *The Counselling of Jesus* (Hodder and Stoughton: London, 1985).

Michael Mitton, *The Wisdom to Listen* (Grove Booklets: Bramcote, 1981).

David Augsburger, *Caring Enough to Confront* (Marshall-Pickering: Basingstoke, 1985).

Alistair Ross, *A Shoulder to Cry On* (UCCF Booklets: Leicester, 1988).

# 8

## *Counselling the Depressed Person*

Not everyone is able to be a counsellor, but if we find ourselves working with someone there are four important areas to be aware of.

1. Discover what the person wants. The person may not know, but because we have listened we may be able to point to things they have said that give some kind of indication of what they want. A depressed person writes, 'A very important part of getting well, besides the acceptance of the fact that you are ill, is to really want to get well.' Having reached this point the next stage is being willing to want to change. Some people would rather remain with a problem that gives them some kind of attention than have it dealt with and face anonymity. The same person wrote, 'Depression had become a habit, an excuse for not taking any responsibility for my life. It was also an attempt to draw attention to myself when I felt that as a normal person I didn't merit any.' All people require attention at some time; that's why children sometimes pretend to be ill. One little girl announced to her mum at break-

fast that she had measles and was covered in spots. Unfortunately she had used a green felt-pen. It is more helpful to encourage a willingness to change and then find more appropriate ways of meeting this 'childlike' need for attention.

2. Assuming the person does want to change, the next problem is, how? In the course of listening we should be looking for patterns that link events to the onset of depression. Paul was frequently depressed. As I had listened to his story it appeared that every time he came into conflict with authority figures he became depressed. I asked him about his father and he told me that his father was a very authoritarian person to whom everyone gave in. This made Paul angry, but he did not dare express anger to his father. In fact it seemed that this anger provoked Paul to challenge authority figures, but always left him feeling depressed and a failure as he really wanted to challenge his father and never felt able to. Paul had been aware of this problem but had never linked it to his depression.

Often the person is aware of something that they believe to be the cause of the depression, but they will only tell us when they sufficiently trust us. As every person is different, what would almost guarantee depression in one person, can be coped with easily by others.

3. Depression, anger and problems to do with expressing anger are commonly linked. Christians often have problems with anger, yet God is described as being angry over 400 times. Jesus became angry with the Pharisees and his own disci-

ples (Mk 3:5, 10:13–16). Expressed in depression, anger has become destructive but:

> Anger can be used positively and creatively if it is seen as a warning signal that things are amiss in personal or social relationships, and if its arousing effect is used to promote honest and direct communication with those causing the hurt and frustration.[7]

As a carer you need to be able to face hostility and rejection vented upon you by a depressed person. They need to know that we are 'safe' people who will not throw it back at them in their vulnerability. Part of dealing with and moving out of the depression will be the willingness to express uncomfortable and difficult things to someone they trust. A carer needs the expertise to draw these feelings and emotions out.

4. As we are involved in caring it is important that we too have someone who will help, direct or supervise us. When working with depressed people it is not unusual to experience a degree of depression oneself, and skill is needed to help us disentangle what we experience from what we listen to. Anger focused upon us is not easy, and it may awaken personal issues that we may not have resolved.

Often the most difficult time for a carer is when despite all the hard work the person does not get any better. We can feel as if we have failed. Some of the people who do this caring are pastors who are used to coming up with the answers. As a pastor I can say that pastors often need help but are often bad at asking for it. It seems to imply failure. Such a step is a recognition of strength rather than weakness.

## Further reading

Alastair Campbell, *The Gospel of Anger* (SPCK: London, 1986).

Mary Pytches, *A Healing Fellowship* (Hodder and Stoughton: London, 1988).

Michael Jacobs, *Still Small Voice. An introduction to Counselling* (SPCK: London, 1982).

Gary Collins, *Christian Counselling* Revised edition (Word Publishing: Dallas, 1988).

# 9

## *Spurgeon on Depression*

Charles Haddon Spurgeon, writing over a century ago describes how he experienced depression and how he coped with it. He is a good example of showing us that there is life during depression and after it. Spurgeon was a famous and popular Victorian preacher, pastor of six-thousand members and founder of a theological college. He also established an orphanage, a clothing society, a temperance organisation, an evangelistic society, homes for the elderly and three mission halls. Spurgeon was also the author of numerous pamphlets and one-hundred and fifty-three books, as well as being editor of a monthly magazine. Yet Spurgeon had to cope with depression. In a sermon he said, 'There are experiences of the children of God which are full of spiritual darkness; and I am almost persuaded that those of God's servants who have been most highly favoured have, nevertheless, suffered more times of darkness than others.' [9] Very few saw the private cost of such a renowned preaching ministry. In the vestry before a service,

Spurgeon would often be in a state of great anxiety, pacing up and down, pale and sometimes even being physically sick.[10] After the service,

> he frequently had to contend with a severe depressive reaction.... On these occasions Mrs Susannah Spurgeon would read poetry to him, or page after page of Baxter's Reformed Pastor, feeling his grief and attempting the comfort of 'quiet sympathy'. Sometimes the great preacher was so overcome by phases of melancholy that he would resort to a rented chalet on the South Downs accompanied by Pastor William Upton, his trusted confidant, in whose company the worst of the crisis would be conquered.[11]

If he had been alive today he would have found great help in the treatment available. He describes the effect of depression in spiritual terms, showing again his remarkable understanding of human nature and his confidence in his Almighty God. In one of his lectures to his students Spurgeon wrote:

> Knowing by most painful experience what deep depression of spirit means...I thought it might be consolatory...if I gave my thoughts thereon, that younger men might not fancy that some strange things has happened to them when they become for a season possessed by melancholy.[12]

Spurgeon mentions five reasons why we may suffer from depression.

First, because we are human and we live in a complex, hostile and painful world. Depression is part of our history as the human race. 'Is any man altogether sane? Are we not all a little off balance?

Some minds appear to have a gloomy tinge essential to their very individuality.' [13]

Secondly, the pressures of caring for and leading others makes us vulnerable. 'This loneliness...is a fertile source of depression,' added to 'a heart burdened with many cares, and we have all the elements for preparing a seething cauldron of despair, especially in the dim months of fog.' [14] Through long periods of demanding work it is possible to work oneself into the ground and into depression.

Thirdly, what other people think about us and expect from us. This was a constant pressure for Spurgeon; even his very success caused him to be depressed. 'The curtain was rising on my lifework and I dreaded what it might reveal.... My success appalled me.... Excess of joy or excitement must be paid for by subsequent depressions.' [15]

Fourthly, sudden setbacks. Spurgeon was so popular as a preacher that a Music Hall in the Royal Surrey Gardens was booked, which sat 12,000 people. The hall was packed to capacity when someone shouted out 'fire'. In the ensuing panic, seven people died in the crush even though there never had been a fire. The effect on Spurgeon was immense and life-long. 'At first these things utterly stagger us, and send us to our homes wrapped in a horror of great darkness.... The tumult, the panic, the deaths were day and night before me and made life a burden.' [16]

Fifthly, 'This evil will come upon us, we know not why, and then it is all the more difficult to drive away. Causeless depression is not to be reasoned with... as well as fight with the mist as with this shapeless, undefinable, yet all-beclouding hopelessness.' [17]

Having examined a wide range of causes, Spurgeon had no easy answers. His first encouragement was simply to accept it as part of life and realise that feelings are not the whole story. Take a day at a time, and live it hour by hour. The second was to ask that God would release us and protect us. 'The iron bolt which so mysteriously fastens the door of hope and holds our spirits in gloomy prison, needs a heavenly hand to push it back.' [18] Spurgeon achieved a remarkable amount in his life and that is even more impressive when we consider the depths and frequency of his depression. Though we may not be gifted in quite the same way as Spurgeon, he gives us hope if we suffer from depression and hope for those whom we counsel, care for and support.

# Notes

[1] Gary Collins, *Christian Counselling. A Comprehensive Guide* Revised edition (Word: Dallas, 1988), p 105.

[2] Ibid, p 106.

[3] Rowland Moss, 'Stress and Depression—a personal experience', *Christian Arena*, (June 1984): p 12.

[4] See 'Bearing one another's burdens', in Alistair Ross', *A Shoulder to Cry On* (UCCF Booklets: Leicester, 1988).

[5] Quoted in Selwyn Hughes, *A Friend in Need* (Kingsway: Eastbourne, 1981), p 49.

[6] Anonymous, 'Depression—A personal view', *Counselling*, vol 51 (February 1985): p 18.

[7] Ibid, p 17.

[8] Alastair Campbell, 'Anger and Hostility', *A Dictionary of Pastoral Care* (SPCK: London, 1987), p 14.

[9] Peter Masters, 'A Pastoral Approach to the Burden of Depression', *Sword and Trowel*, (May 1989): p 23.

[10] Eric Hayden, *A Centennial History of Spurgeon's Tabernacle* (Clifford Frost: London, 1962), p 10.

[11] Masters, ibid.

[12] C. H. Spurgeon, *Lectures to my Students* (Passmore and Alabaster: London, 1890) p 167.

[13] Ibid, p 168.

[14] Ibid, p 171.

[15] Ibid, p 173.

[16] Ibid, p 175.

[17] Ibid, p 177.

[18] Ibid.

# Helpful Books on Depression

Chave-Jones, Myra. *Coping with Depression*. Lion: Tring, 1981.
An eighty page gold mine which you could give to a depressed person.
—*Listening to your feelings*. Lion: Tring, 1989.
This is for anyone thinking about their own needs and whether or not they may be able to help others.

Davies, Gaius. *Stress, The Challenge to Christian Caring*. Kingsway: Eastbourne, 1988.
This is a wide ranging sourcebook of psychiatric and biblical advice.

Foyle, Marjory. *Honourably Wounded. Stress among Christian Workers*. MARC: Eastbourne, 1987.
Years of missionary experience and psychiatric training combine to encourage the care of missionaries.

Hurding, Roger. *Coping with Illness*. Hodder and Stoughton: London, 1987.
A more general book on illness with a helpful Bible study on Job.

Lawson, Michael. *Facing Depression*. Hodder and Stoughton: London, 1989.
This contains much helpful material, particularly a series of questions, exercises and prayers.

Lloyd-Jones, Martyn. *Spiritual Depression*. Pickering and Inglis: Glasgow, 1965.
This covers what causes us to fail as Christians and so become spiritually depressed.

Rowe, Dorothy. *Depression, the Way Out of your Prison*. RKP: London, 1983.
A stimulating book looking at depression from a fresh perspective and raising challenging questions.

White, John. *The Masks of Melancholy. A Christian psychiatrist looks at depression and suicide*. IVP: Leicester, 1982.
Contains helpful material on suicide and the demonic.

Winter, Richard. *The Roots of Sorrow. Reflections on Depression and Hope*. Paternoster Press: Exeter, 1988.
Wide-ranging and informative.

# Spurgeon's Booklet Series

Also in this series:

*Pastors Under Pressure*
by Paul Beasley Murray, series editor and Principle of Spurgeon's College in London. He draws upon his thirteen years in pastoral ministry to provide an invaluable understanding of how church leaders and their congregations can together overcome the stress so crippling to pastors.

*The Activist's Guide to Prayer*
by Brian Gilbert - himself a Baptist Minister and Christian activist - is written for those whose busyness threatens to squeeze out the prayer that is so vital for effective ministry. The author shares insights which will help other activists give priority to prayer.

*The Authority of Scripture*
by Andrew Rigden Green, brings together the most salient points in the debate about Scripture with refreshing clarity and sharp observations. The author, who is Senior Pastor of Upton Vale Baptist Church in Torquay, offers here a most helpful guide to anyone wanting to defend the Bible's authority.

*Small Groups in the Church*
by Keith Roberts, pastor of Mitcham Lane Baptist Church in South London, is a practical tool for ministers and leaders within the growing network of small groups in the church. Full of practical suggestions and common sense to encourage nurture and growth.

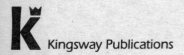

Kingsway Publications